We Don't Want to Play

by

Andrew Brattrud

4075 Twining St. Riverside CA 92509

Edited by Kathleen "Tina" Brown

www.RiversideChristianAssembly.com

Audio versions of the lesson are available on the RCA app

TABLE OF CONTENTS

Introduction

Two rats meet, running through the wall of a dilapidated house. They wouldn't know it, but one was the great uncle of the other. Big. Fat. Strong. Scary. Well learned. There was something familiar in the other for each of them. It was not hostile or threatening, but they began to wrestle. The older pinned the other, then let him up. Then again. But on the third time, the uncle rat rolled over at first contact. The little nephew sprang up and pinned him. Joy. Triumph. A bit of exhaustion. They would look forward to seeing each other again. There would be many more matches. Rats are social animals. They love to play. They love to play so much that the bigger ones will sometimes allow the little ones to win. If they just won every time, the little ones would never play. That would be the worst insult.

There are too many games. We wear too many costumes. We can say to this world "I don't want to play."

RCA

4075 Twining St. Riverside, Ca 92509

False Centers

Jim Carrey chipped his tooth to play the legendary role of Lloyd Christmas in *Dumb and Dumber (1)*. Academy Award winner Adrien Brody lost 30 pounds, dropping him to 130 for his role in *The Pianist*. He sold his car and apartment (2). Some roles are consuming, some roles are disturbing. The Joker is one such notorious part. Jared Leto gave a live rat to co-star Margot Robbie, a dead pig to the entire cast, and bullets to Will Smith— all the while pretending to be the Joker off set (3). They did not appreciate his antics. Previous to Jared, Heath Ledger got lost in the darkness of the character. For almost six weeks he locked himself in a hotel to practice the laugh, voice and mannerisms

(4). He would purposely deprive himself of sleep. It was a taxing role he would not finish.

"Acting is not about being someone different. It's finding the similarity in what is apparently different, then finding myself in there," stated legendary actress Meryl Streep (5).

Who are the most famous people in the world? Politicians? Scientists? Doctors? Preachers? No. We love our actors. Dwayne "The Rock" Johnson is one of the most famous people in the world, in the top five on every list. He wins in the square circle and he wins in action movies.

John Cena, another wrestler-turned-actor, often voices commercials. He tells us to buy a Honda, eat pistachios and get a credit check with Experian. Why? Why would we listen to him about these products? He is not speaking from his heart, but from his bank account. He is not speaking from his soul or his mind or his center, but he *acts* like he is.

Actor Peter Bergman played Dr. Cliff Warner on the popular soap opera "All My Children." He was so trusted that Vicks Formula 44 hired him for their 1986 commercial where he famously said, "I am not a doctor, but I play one on TV (6)." I guess that is enough for people's trust. We love our pretenders because we are pretenders. Those with false centers admire those with famous "false centers."

"Whoever hates dissembles himself with his lips, lying up deceit within him. When he speaks fair, do not believe him for there are seven abominations in his heart. Whose hatred is covered by deceit, his wickedness shall be shewed before the whole congregation." Proverbs 26:24-26.

There are too many false centers because of **disguises**, **dissembling** and **deception**. We need integrity, unity and the truth.

"Deceit in the heart devises evil, but counselors of peace have joy," Proverbs 12:20. When we announced that the money for a new playground for the kids had come in, the whole congregation cheered. Even those adults who will never use the swings. We love our community. Potlucks, flag football clinics, free karate, and our basketball league all garner support. We love to think about those things. Good things. But the wicked are not so. They meditate on revenge, on lust, and on greed. Their fantasy life is full of sin. Their center is dark.

Have you ever taken someone to lunch and insisted "I got the bill—get whatever you want," and no sooner did you say it, that you regretted it? They put down the "lunch specials" menu and pick up the regular one. There go the $9.95 options. "Can I get you something to drink?" Quickly, you declare for water, hoping they will follow. "I'll have a Coke." Cha-ching your mind rings. There goes $3.99 and you hope they have free refills. "Can I start you with an appetizer?" Before you can say "No thanks," your friend blurts out "onion rings." There may be a smile on your face, but your center is doing sad math. He keeps track. "'Eat and drink,' he says to you, but his heart is not with you." Proverbs 23:7.

The Bible is filled with great actors. Cain played a role. After murdering his brother, God confronted him. "Where is Abel?" "I don't know, am I my brother's keeper?" He wanted to be someone else.

The greatest actor in the scripture must be King David's General Joab. Twice he played the friendly supporter, when he was really the jealous, vindictive killer. Abner had killed Joab's brother in a battle. He had led Ishbosheth's army against David. When he wanted to defect, he met with David under peaceful conditions. But when he left, Joab saw him and followed him outside the city. With a wave and a smile, he disarmed Abner. As they embraced, he stabbed him under the fifth rib. Years later, he repeated the kind-guy-killer and did the same to Amasa, a general that tried to take his job.

"The man who walks in integrity, walks securely." Proverbs 10:9.

Robert Downey Jr. was Iron Man for over a decade, earning him millions of dollars. But after the death of the character, rumors have him returning as the villain, Dr. Doom. Similar things happened to the actor Micheal B. Jordan, who played Human

Torch in one film, and then was Erik Killmonger in another. Chris Evans was Human Torch before him, and then became Captain America. How? They just change costumes and voices, and the actors change their center. Another false one.

Because of Disguises

"For there are many false apostles and deceitful workers, transforming themselves into the apostles of Christ. It is not surprising, for Satan himself is transformed into an angel of light." (2 Corinthians 11:13-15.) Many preachers want your money. Some are egomaniacs. Some have nefarious motives. With fresh haircuts every other week, fashion show clothes and the trendiest sneakers, they look the part. Charisma, knowledge and a presence, but no substance. No Holy Spirit power. No true center, only lots of frills.

Adam and Eve sinned. They realized they were naked and quickly got a costume change. Fig leaves covered them. They hid. God found them. Hide-and-Go-Seek against God is a short game.

King Ahab had been warned. "You will lose the battle. You will never return. Death is waiting for you," the prophet declared. Instead of his royal outfit, he called in another wardrobe and changed up his look. His kingly chariot was replaced with soldiers. He wanted to play "Guess Who" with God. In the battle, a random arrow struck him between the joints of the foot soldier's armor. As he bled out in the chariot, he could only lament his silly play. God saw him. "No one can hide from the Almighty," Habakkuk echoed.

Rather than hiding from God, we should be "hidden in Christ," as Colossians 3:3 states. My behavior is not what the legislators pass. My ethics, my principles and my beliefs are all from Heaven. That is where my center is.

Mick Foley was one of WWE's most popular wrestlers. He loved the sport and the fans loved him. He played three different characters: "Mankind," the relentless, aggressive glutton for punishment; "Cactus Jack," a hardcore wild man; and "Dude Love," a loving hippie. It was January 18, 1998 in San Jose, California the scene for the Royal Rumble. Many would enter, but only one would be there at the end. If you were thrown from the ring, you were eliminated. About every 90 seconds, another man entered the ring. The crowd went nuts when Cactus Jack entered the event. He was going hard, punching, kicking and looking for his slams, until Chainsaw Charlie tossed him out. The crowd booed! A few minutes later, there was a roar through the bleachers as Mankind's music came on. Mick was back with a new costume. He had momentum. His aggressiveness was evident. He was like a man possessed, until he, too, was put out. The crowd booed again. But then, minutes later, Dude Love's theme music was on. Mick was back...again. He went to war, but was eliminated by The Rock. Three times.

Three characters. Three disguises. Three losses (7). Why did he keep changing? It is the same reason *we* change, but why do we keep changing? We don't want to be that person anymore.

The apostate King Jeroboam had one good son. He had one son that feared God, and the others were apostates like their father. The prince became sick. Jeroboam was ashamed to seek God, because he had built golden calves after God visited him, so he sent his wife to visit a seer. Before she went, she put on a costume. But right away, the seer was not deceived. "God sees you. He sees your sick son. Something good has been found in him, so he will die as soon as you reenter the city. He will get an honorable burial. He will be spared what will happen to you and the rest of your family. You will die in the fields and be eaten by dogs." As soon as she crossed the gates, her son perished. She wore a costume because she did not want to be the sinful mother of a sick child; she wanted to be someone else.

King Saul was told he was going to die in battle. Without someone to console him, he put on a disguise and visited a witch. She conjured the spirit of Samuel. "If God said you are going to die, oh, you are going to die!"—Samuel rebuked from the grave. The witch knew it was him. Why was he hiding? It is the same reason we hide: we are ashamed, and hate the bad news that hangs over us.

King Herod wanted Jesus to play. Pontus Pilate knew Jesus was innocent. He saw through the sham of a midnight trial. The condition of Jesus' beaten face was evidence of their injustice. Plus, his wife had a dream about the innocent man. "Have nothing to do with him," she pleaded. Perhaps he thought a violent scourging would pacify the crowd. Thirty-nine times, that leather, rock and glass whip tore through Jesus. His back was shredded. "That ought to be enough." No. They wanted His life. Pilate was put in a bad position. The peer pressure. The threats of allowing an "insurrectionist" to go free. Like a lightning bolt, he saw his out. King Herod happened to be in Jerusalem. He governed where Jesus was from. He could have jurisdiction.

Herod was an odd man. Fancy. Immature. Decadent. For a long time, he wanted to meet Jesus. He had heard about the miracles and the masses. "Oh boy! Oh boy! The magic man has come to entertain me!" Roman soldiers brought a bloody Jesus to Herod. "Do a trick. Do a trick!" He demanded. Turn this dirty water into pure wine…I'm thirsty!" Jesus just sat there. "Oh, I know, I know. Heal yourself. Close your bloody back." Nothing from Jesus. "This is the new king? He is a bloody mess. Worse. He is bloody boring." In jest, one of the soldiers gathered some thorns and wove them into a circle. "Here I have a crown for the king." They pressed it deep into His skin. Joining the fun, another soldier found an old purple garment a royal had left at the lost and found. "Here, here, dress Him up." With a smile, another grabbed a scepter. "Watch this." He smashed it into Jesus' ribs, "Your majesty!" Herod roared with glee. "A king, a king, the king of the Jews!" They laughed. But Jesus did not laugh. He did not take on the roll. He did not play the part. He did not come to be their entertainment. He came to die and be risen. To complete their pretend game, they sat Jesus in the seat of judgement and bowed to Him. "What is your decree?" Jesus, with a crown, royal purple and a scepter, sitting in the seat of the governor, was the only one not playing.

The worst insult is when you stop playing and just go home.

We need integrity. "Let your yes be your yes," Jesus commanded. Be who you are at church, at home, at school, at work and in the dark or the light, be the same. You only have one soul. It is always with you. The condition of that soul is going to tell all of your life. "If your eyes are pure, everything is pure." "Integrity guards the way of the upright," Proverbs 11:3 reminds us. Walk securely. Jesus was who He was and is who He is.

Because of Disassembly

Imagine getting your kids the Lego Star Wars Millennium Falcon. It set you back almost $900. For weeks, you build together. Brick by brick. Each detail is set in its perfect place. Finally, it is complete! Then they have their cousin come over and start playing Legos. They need a piece and one from the Falcon just happens to be perfect. "Noooooo!" you're thinking. You know once they start taking pieces, they are not coming back. It is getting disassembled.

"The one that hates disassembles…"

You can try to compartmentalize, but once the root of bitterness enters your heart, your center, it is difficult to get it out. Once lust enters, it wants to be fulfilled. You can try to say "Well, I'm only that way when no one is around," or "it doesn't hurt anyone if they don't know," but that is not integrity. That is pulling yourself apart.

The Book of Hebrews warns us against those who leave the assembling together. Backsliding. Overcome by sin. It would be better if they never believed. To get pieced up is devastating.

The early church had inner turmoil. Paul's letter to the Galatians describes the conflict he had with the Apostle Peter. Peter, of whom the Lord said "I will build my church upon this rock," the same Peter who preached on Pentecost to 3000 converts, yes, that Peter was playing the hypocrite. He was playing two roles. Jesus was Jewish, as were all the original disciples. They kept the laws of Moses and the Holy days. But in Acts chapter 10, we see the gentiles (non-Jewish people), are allowed to get water baptized, take communion and are filled with the Holy Spirit. It was determined that they did not have to become "Jewish" to become a Christian. Much of their culture stayed the same, including most of their diet. Peter saw their freedom and he would join them for meals. He is enjoying pulled pork sandwiches and shrimp skewers for the first time, but when the Jewish Christian leaders would come into town, he would refuse the gentile food. He was one way with some of them and another way with the others. "I rebuked him to his face for playing the hypocrite. Even Barnabus was brought into this disassembly," Paul records.

There are many reasons people backslide. They at one point wanted to be close to Christ and part of His body, but part of them changes. Then more of them changes. The seesaw of desire gets heavier and heavier, until it switches. I am not surprised when I hear of big-named preachers or Christian leaders falling into sin. Sin is alluring. It feels good. It must, for people to do it. But it has such terrible consequences. You can lose your marriage, relationship with your kids, your wealth, and your health for momentary pleasures, but the pleasures can be screaming at you. "Pray that you do not fall into temptation," Jesus commanded. "We are drawn away by our own desires," the Apostle James describes. Part of us wants a new role, a new character, one that is a hedonist.

August 12, 1985, Japan Airlines Flight 123 had left Tokyo's Haneda Airport and was headed to Osaka. Seven years earlier, there had been an improper repair. A fuel line was damaged and was leaking. Slow leaks can lead to disasters. The crash would kill 520 out of the 524 (8). You have some leaks. You need to be "being filled with the Holy Spirit." This week, you will spend time with some emotional vampires. You will have some taxing and tolling people. You are light in a dark place. It can weary us, so we need to constantly be turning to Jesus.

The woman with the issue of blood, stretched out and grabbed the hem of Jesus' garment. "Virtue went out of Him." Something left Him.

Lot's soul was vexed by simply being in Sodom. The perversion was vile. The poor were being oppressed. Suffering. Babies crying by themselves. Kids with bloated bellies. Men with wicked intentions. It was evil. Within him there was a constant alarm going off, "this is bad." Something was being taken from him. This world is like that. It will drain you and try to disassemble you.

We need unity. Unity within our self. It is a warning when someone says "I am being my true self." That is like declaring "my truth." There is an objective reality. Some will say "my body is male, but my soul is female." This is a disassembly.

Because of Deception

"I marvel that you are so quickly turned to 'another' gospel. One that is not a gospel at all," the Apostle Paul wrote to the Galatian church. They had been deceived.

"If you say you have no sin, you deceive yourself," John would later write. "Self-deception is still deception. Lying to yourself is still lying. "Do not deceive yourself; whatsoever a man sows, the same he will reap," Paul told the Galatians. Life has surprises, but the harvest really should not be one of them. If you have done well, expect good. If you have lived sinfully, expect judgement.

There is so much deception that we are called to "test the spirits." Many are imposters. In these last days, they grow worse and worse. The "false prophets" and "wolves" Jesus warned us about are here. They are wearing "sheep's clothing." The wheat and the tares look similar for a while, but in the end, they are separated. The sheep and the goats may look similar, but they, too, are separated in the end.

Your faith is the prize that God and Satan are contending over. Will you put your faith in Jesus and receive His righteousness? Or will you keep your faith in yourself and this world which is perishing?

The truth centers us.

We need the truth. "I am the way, the truth and the life," Jesus declared. We need Jesus. "You shall know the truth and the truth shall set you free," Jesus taught. It is the belt of truth that holds us together.

Many actors are playing roles on our TV. There is a popular show that has no actors and has no script. It is reality. Have you ever watched "Hoarders?" It takes you inside the homes and minds of people who struggle with a mental disorder that results in them compulsively buying and keeping massive amounts of objects. Their houses are literally piles of trash. I remember seeing one episode that struck me. There was a women who had so much to lose. She was the mother of two embarrassed teenagers and the wife of a husband who was not sure how much longer he could put up with her compulsions. "I felt like my mother was choosing her garbage over us," one of the teenagers confessed. They had never had friends come over. There was shame. Now, she allowed the camera crews to come in. Roaches and rats were scurrying. There was mold everywhere and disgusting, filled toilets. It was disturbing. Paths were made around the piles. Most of the house was useless storage. But the mom wanted to change. Her filth was exposed. She was herself. Her bad habits, her anxiety, and her brokenness was all on display. Tears. Yells. But she wanted to change. The Hoarders crew came through and emptied the house. It was dump truck after dump truck of items. Some things were given to charity, a few things were kept, but most of it went to the landfill. She had a part in the decisions being made. A professional counselor was there to help. She would go to therapy. Her kids wept with joy. Her husband squeezed her with tears of relief. He was getting his life back! She was not an actress, but she was on TV. She was herself; messy, shameful and problematic, but once she confessed, she was able to change. The outside of the house always looked good. It was a good act. It was the inside that needed attention.

We are all like that. Filthy on the inside, but good looking on the outside. Stop acting.

"Acting is emotional athletics...it is pain," to quote Al Pacino (9). The liar has a lot to account for. They will get exhausted keeping their stories straight.

You were only made with one soul. You were made to live with integrity, unity and the truth.

Conclusion

My friend Rev. Manny and his wife Gracie love Jesus and hate the devil. During our Halloween outreach, they made a piñata in the shape of Satan. I thought it was a funny sentiment to have kids whapping his red horned head with sticks and bats. Strike after strike, but no candy fell. You could hear the rumbling. It was weighty. They had taped it super well. Whap after whap! Finally, the exhausted, excited kids saw what looked to be a tear in the piñata. "Let the big kids have a shot!" A youth with the thickest moustache stepped forward. He was a varsity baseball player. "Get ready kids…" One massive swing, and both of the devil's Paper Mache legs went flying. Kids rushed it. It was a frenzy. But no candy. No toys. Only, literally, dust and pebbles.

It was filled with dirt! The adults laughed. The kids looked terrified. "The devil is a liar!" Rev. Manny yelled. With that, all the surrounding adults starting throwing their hidden candy into the air for the kids to chaotically collect. It was awesome. The devil is a deceiver. He promises and does not deliver.

This world is passing away. Do not think you can cash in all of its promises. Be centered on Christ. There are many false prophets, many charlatans and sheep in wolves' clothing waiting to devour you. Be on guard. Compare everything to God's word.

You are indwelt by the Holy Spirit. You have the mind of Christ. The gift of discernment is yours. Use it.

How sad it would be to be excited about hitting the center of a target only to find you hit the wrong target. It's like you bowled a strike, but you're in the wrong lane. Before you start a journey, know your destination. Before you start work, know what the master is asking. Your definition of "good" is not good. Your concept of what God values is likely skewed. You may be running fast in the wrong the direction. Good form. Good follow-through. But you will lose.

Don't be misguided. The Holy Spirit is called to be our Guide. He is with you. Disguises and costumes won't do. We don't play dress-up or hide-and-seek like Adam and Eve did. We live with integrity, unity and the truth.

References:

1. How Jim Carrey chipped his tooth for 'Dumb and Dumber', Arun Starkey, aug18, 2022
2. Oscar nom Adrien Brody on 'The Pianist', Adam Duerson, Jan13, 2003
3. The gifts Jared Leto sent to his co-stars on 'Suicide Squad', Poppy Burton, Sept2, 2023
4. Heath ledger hid away in a motel room for about six weeks to prepare for his role as the joker during this time ledger delved deep into the psychology of the character | The Fact Base, Morgan Wallace, feb2, 2024
5. Fixquotes.com
6. Peter Bergman - Wikipedia
7. Royal Rumble (1998) - Wikipedia
8. Japan Air Lines Flight 123 - Wikipedia
9. Brainyquote.com

www.ingramcontent.com/pod-product-compliance
Lightning Source LLC
Chambersburg PA
CBHW071811020426
42331CB00008B/2458